Listen With your Heart,
Cindy W. Beard

His Messages

CINDY WALL BEARD

WINEPRESS WP PUBLISHING

Printed in the United States of America
Cover photo by Milton Morris Photogaphy.

Verses marked KJV are taken from the King James Version of the Bible.

Packaged by WinePress Publishing, PO Box 1406, Mukilteo, WA 98275. The views expressed or implied in this work do not necessarily reflect those of WinePress Publishing. Ultimate design, content, and editorial accuracy of this work is the responsibility of the author(s).

ISBN 1-57921-117-8
Library of Congress Catalog Card Number: 97-60608

DEDICATION

Thank You, Lord, for the gift of salvation and the words to express Your awesome deeds in my life. You, Lord, are the true author of this book. I thank You for the privilege of being the vessel You chose in this work for Your glory.

I want to express my love and appreciation to my cheerleaders who encouraged me daily to complete this book—my parents, William and Barbara Wall. Both of you made this vision a reality. I thank God daily for handpicking you to be my parents. I am truly blessed.

To Reid and Shawn, my precious children, thank you for believing in your mama and being so understanding. Both of you are gifts from God.

To my tall, handsome husband, Avery. We have shared the joy of the mountaintop experiences with the Lord, as well as the struggles and tears in the valleys of trouble. Through it all we have held on to the Anchor of Hope, Jesus. I love you and thank you.

There is a special man I want to thank, my papa. You have always seen the best in me, and I love you. God gave you a vision of this book long before it became a fulfilled prophecy. Thank you for your prayers and belief.

To all the prayer warriors who prayed for this work to bring glory to God and who covered me in a blanket of prayers, thank you.

To all of you I dedicate this work in honor of God, for His glory.

CONTENTS

Foreword

Although each person's daily walk with God follows a road perhaps traveled differently by others, we can learn and encourage others to keep their eyes on Jesus, the Author and Finisher of our faith. If one person has demonstrated this statement over the last six years, it has been Cindy Beard.

Cindy and her husband, Avery, first came to me a little over six years ago, searching for a new direction. Through a time of spiritual guidance and self-examination they found the key to life: a relationship with Jesus Christ. I will never forget the day that Cindy shared the joy of accepting Christ. Her excitement in accepting Christ overshadowed the news that she shared with me next. Her doctor had called that morning, just hours after she had given her heart to Christ, with the verdict of cancer.

I must confess that my heart was overwhelmed with the joy of her salvation, but I was stunned by the news of her disease. But, more specifically, I was stunned at God's perfect timing for her life and the power of God's Holy Spirit to give her the courage to face this news with a positive attitude and the certainty that "in all things Christ will be glorified."

Over the next years I saw Cindy exemplify her faith through good times and bad: the trials of enduring chemotherapy and its painful side effects; the agony of having to wait for test results and hoping the cancer was in remission; the euphoria of hearing her doctors say the cancer was in remission, only to be devastated a short time later with the appearance of new tumors. The real mark of faith is staying in the race; and Cindy ran the obstacle course through pain, fear, frustration, and uncertainty but never gave up on the hope that she found in Christ.

Through it all she learned to trust in God. Through speaking and prayer, Cindy has used the gifts that God gave her. She has shared her testimony in churches all over our state and others. She has a true gift for sharing God's love, which grabs the attention of those who are trying to put the pieces of their lives back together.

God has also blessed Cindy with the gift of intercession. She has spent many hours in intercessory prayer for people in her church, community, and all over the state. The power of prayer is illustrated best in Cindy's own pilgrimage. I cannot count the number of times God has interceded in this lady's life, and she is still telling the story that "Christ is triumphant and He wants us to be alive and well."

I feel very fortunate to have served as the pastor and friend of this lady. My own faith has been strengthened and often times paled in comparison to Cindy's. The things that I so easily allow to beset me are minuscule compared to the battles Cindy and others with devastating diseases face with courage and faith each day.

As you read her poems and personal stories in this book may it help you define the "joykillers" in your life, and may the inspiration from Cindy's story give you the faith to believe that God can give you the power to bring triumph from tragedy.

CAREY MCELVEEN
Pastor of The First Baptist Church
Pageland, SC

Introduction

My Lord started preparing me for this work on August 4, 1993, at 1:00 A.M. He became Lord of my life and gave me my first message, "The Greatest Invitation." Since that moment He has inspired me to write and has given me many experiences to share. When I asked Him how I would compile everything, He provided a computer within two weeks. When I questioned if this was truly the work He had called me to do, He always confirmed it through His children by having them ask me if I would write a book. Once when I spoke at a church, a very precious preacher said, "Cindy, you can't be everywhere at one time to share your story. I think God has called you to write a book so more people can be ministered to." In 1996, after a three-year battle with cancer, my doctor thought the cancer had spread to my throat. As I was dressing for my appointment, I heard God speak to me loud and clear. The words I heard were, "Do I have to take your voice for you to write?" I fell to my knees, crying out to God, "No, I'll write it. Help me, Lord. I will finish the work."

The day after I had asked God who would publish this book, I read an article about Athena and Chuck Dean, the founders of WinePress Publishing. Two weeks later I heard Athena Dean on a Christian radio program. Then in July 1997, I met the precious Deans in Atlanta, Georgia. I knew the Lord had ordained the trip and appointed the meeting. Isn't God awesome?!

His Messages has been a joy journey that began over four years ago, and I pray His messages will speak to you and take you on a journey with Him. Listen. He is speaking to you.

MESSAGES

I never know when the Lord
Will inspire me to write.
His messages come during sweet
Fellowship, and He wakes me
During the night.
He ever so softly whispers the thought
That witnesses to my soul,
Line by line He guides my mind
Until the message is told.
These blessings come in the form of poems
And I believe they are meant to share.
To touch a heart, to bring a smile,
To remind people that God still cares.
So when you hear a poem, and it
Truly speaks to your heart,
Just think God may have had you in
Mind from the very start.

These are the scriptures the Lord gave to encourage me to pen *His Messages*:

My heart is overflowing with a good matter; I speak of
the things which I have made touching the King. My
tongue is the pen of a ready writer. (Ps. 45:1)

The Lord God hath given me the tongue of the learned,
that I should know how to speak a word in season to him
who is weary: He wakeneth morning by morning, He
wakeneth mine ear to hear as the learned. (Isa. 50:4)

I pray you will be encouraged by the Holy Spirit and
that He will directly minister to your needs. Listen as He
softly speaks to you. You may have been the reason the
Lord inspired me to write *His Messages.* Encounter His touch
and experience His grace. Jesus loves you. Always remember
through every trial, all adversity, if He brought you to
it, He will see you through it. Anything that touches your
life went through God's hands first, and He knows what is
best. He promises to always be with you and to work all
things together for your good.

Seeds of Salvation

One sunny afternoon while sitting at my friend Cindi's kitchen table, I listened as she talked about Jesus. Her words painted a picture of love and friendship, and I soon realized I didn't know Him in that way. My heart screamed, *You only know of Him.*

Then she excitedly talked about her desire for His soon return. That totally frightened me, and at that moment, I knew I didn't know Him as my Savior. I was not ready for His return. I knew I would be left behind if He came. That conversation, that memory, is so vivid in my mind today. Even the smell of her coffee is still fresh. My friend did more than serve coffee that glorious afternoon she planted Kingdom seeds that took root.

I knew the Lord began a work in my heart that very hour. He began to draw me to Him. "For no one can come to me unless the Father who sent me draws him to me" (John 6:44 TLB).

Many months passed as Cindi's words rang over and over in my mind. I began to be more consistent in going to church, and I joined a Bible study group. Then on August 3, 1993, I studied John 8:47: "He that is of God heareth

God's words; ye, therefore, hear them not, because ye are not of God." This scripture was illuminated to my sight, and it pierced my heart. I began crying out to the Lord. I realized I had not taken heed to His word. I knew I had never heard Him speak to me, and I got so scared. I began to work out my own salvation with fear and trembling (Phil. 2:12).

I prayed and prayed through the night. I was so afraid I was in the land of famine, never to hear God call me. Then at 1:10 A.M., on August 4, 1993, I heard these words:

THE GREATEST INVITATION

I have received an invitation I
Cannot refuse.
If I regret this time I will
Surely lose.
I have the opportunity to work with the best.
To be taught by the Leader to
Help lead the rest.
It's a chance of a lifetime with
The ultimate reward.
The gift of eternal life, a love
Relationship with the Lord.
So, I gladly accept the invitation
I receive,
I hear the Lord because I believe.
So, please check your heart if you believe, for
The greatest invitation you will
Ever receive.

The Lord spoke to my heart, and the Holy Spirit flowed through my pen. When the poem of invitation was written,

I accepted His salvation and Jesus came into my heart. "Behold, I stand at the door, and knock: if any man hear my voice, and open the door, I will come in to him, and will sup with him, and he with me" (Rev. 3:20).

Do you know Jesus personally as your Savior, your friend? Have you felt the joy and peace the Holy Spirit brings? My prayer is that if you haven't tasted of the Lord and His goodness, please ask Him to come into your heart now. He is listening and extending the greatest invitation you will ever receive—His salvation. If you know Jesus as your Savior, be a sower and plant seeds.

TESTIFY

Twelve hours from the time I was reborn into the Kingdom of God, I received a telephone call from my gynecologist's office. My pap smear had returned positive, class IV—squamous cell carcinoma. As the nurse spoke these words, my heart pounded. I asked her what this meant, and she paused for what seemed like hours. Then softly she said, "Cancer, Mrs. Beard. You need to come in for a biopsy." I hung up the phone and said out loud, "Lord, I can't have cancer, I'm only thirty-five years old!" Then very gently I heard in reply to my cry, "I saved you twelve hours before." Peace replaced fear and the joy of my salvation returned. I was at work and felt as I needed to be alone with God, so I left.

I rode around talking to the Lord. I said, "Lord I can't die; I don't want to leave my children. I'm too young to die!" At that moment the Holy Spirit brought something back to my memory. For ten years I had worked with the elderly, supplying medical equipment. Over and over I had said, "I don't want to get old." Those words rang out in my head, and I realized that if I didn't grow old, I would have to die young. So immediately, I repented and confessed to

God how sorry I was to have said those words. I did want to live and grow old.

Somehow, I ended up at the house of my pastor, Carey McElveen. When he answered the door, I immediately shared with him about how the Lord saved me twelve hours before. He was so excited; we rejoiced and praised the Lord. In the midst of the joy I told him about the news I had just received from my doctor, and I assured him I would be fine. The Lord's presence was so strong there was little room for sorrow; the joy of the Lord took over. Then my pastor asked me to share all of this in church Sunday. He called it a testimony. I had never done that before, so all I knew was to share my story. I was so excited in the Lord that I agreed to do it. Well, that had been on a Wednesday, and by Sunday morning I was scared to death.

When I started to get dressed that morning, I realized my favorite dress had a hole under the arm. I really wanted to wear the dress, so I decided to wear it anyway and just keep my arm down. I tried to put my contacts in, but they hurt my eyes so badly that I couldn't wear them. So I thought, *No problem. I will wear my glasses.* I put on my glasses and a lens fell out! By this time I was hysterical. I'm very nearsighted, and I knew I wouldn't be able to see a thing. I could not understand why everything was going wrong. I called Cindi, my prayer partner, and told her what was happening. I asked her what to do, and she said laugh. I couldn't believe my ears. I thought, *Laugh?! Huh. Some friend you are.* I was such a baby in Christ that I had no idea she meant to laugh at the devil. I resumed as much composure as I could and said, "Well, Lord, I'm going to church tattered and blind, but I'm going to do it anyway."

The church was packed when I arrived with my family that morning. I believe every member and his brother showed up. Word had gotten out that I had been saved and that I had cancer. Whether out of love, concern, or other reasons, our congregation was full. I sat on my pew and waited to be called. My knees were knocking, and my heart was beating so fast I thought every one could hear me because they kept turning around and smiling. Finally, my moment arrived. I stepped up to the pulpit and said, "Thank you, Jesus."

I couldn't see a single person out there, only vague outlines. What the enemy meant for harm, God used for good. I wasn't scared anymore. I couldn't see if the people were smiling or frowning. I couldn't see them at all. God did more than that. When the invitation for salvation was extended, my husband Avery stepped out, accepted Christ as his Savior, and joined the church. Praise the Lord!

From that second on, I've had a burning desire to tell others about the Lord and what He has done for me, and to encourage them to tell others about Christ Jesus. To get ready!

THE JOURNEY TO HEAVEN

It's a journey of a lifetime with
A Heavenly reward.
It's one trip each and every one
Of us can afford.
It only takes a deposit of your soul.
The Lord then takes us and like
Clay He molds.
With one decision the ticket is

Yours, to do the Lord's work,
To do His chores.
This journey has no limit
On how many can go.
The Lord invites everyone that
Has a desire to do so.
So tell your family, your friends and
Even strangers about the trip.
The Lord wants no one to be overlooked
No one to be skipped.
It's our duty as Christians to
Spread the good news.
The Lord needs all of us for Him to use.
This trip has a guarantee that no one
Will lose.
So get your ticket and spread
The good news.
All aboard! It's time to go.
When you hear the Lord call
Don't tell Him no.
Give Him your soul and you
Are ready to go.

But ye shall receive power, after that the Holy Ghost is come upon you: and ye shall be witnesses unto me both in Jerusalem, and in all Judea, and in Samaria, and unto the uttermost part of the earth. (Acts 1:8)

We all are called to be witnesses for the Lord. Tell someone today what He has done for you. Testify!

PRAYER

The second time I gave my testimony was at a women's prayer group. They passed out a list of names of people they had been praying for—my name was on the list. I knew only one or two people from this church, and thirty or more women were praying for me weekly. I found out they had been praying for me since they had heard I had cancer. I was so touched to know people were interceding on my behalf and believing with me for my healing.

That night on the way home, the Lord began to deal with me about how carelessly I had told people I would pray for them. I always had good intentions, but sometimes I didn't follow through with the prayer as I had promised. He reminded me of the power of prayer and that when people ask me to pray they are saying they have confidence in my prayers. I realized that if I don't pray, I break a promise. I could be the only person they ask to pray.

A PROMISE OF PRAYER

Don't tell someone, "I am praying
For you,"

Unless you really mean it
And follow it through.
Because that person is depending
On you.
And our Lord hears your
Promise too.
How would you feel when that
Person thanks you for your prayer,
And you realized you forgot
Because you really didn't care?
How would you feel if our Lord
Reminds you of this sin?
Would you promise never to
Do it again?
So the next time someone says
"Please remember me in prayer"
Keep your promise, pray for
Them, show our Lord you truly care.

THE POWER OF PRAYER

We are all blessed with a power
One we all share.
It's a gift from our Father
The tool of prayer.
It's our Heavenly line of communication
We must devoutly use.
Without it confusion and temptation
Will surely make us lose.
Our all-knowing Lord knows our
Heart and our intent.
Our sins will be forgiven when

We confess and repent.
All things are possible through God
Just open your heart and pray.
Ask God to do His will for
His purpose, His way.
Never forget our gift, the power
Of prayer. Because Our Lord is the power
And He is everywhere.

The Lord gave me these two poems in 1993 and has burdened my heart to pray for all who ask. I pray I will never again let Him or His children down when I am asked to pray. I try to pray for the need right when it is requested or write it down on a pad I carry, so I won't forget. We never know when we are the only one asked to pray.

I've counted on a lot of prayer during my three battles with cancer, and I know the power of prayer. I'm living proof!

And the prayer of faith shall save the sick, and the Lord shall raise him up. (James 5:15)

Pray one for another. (James 5:16)

Praying always with all prayer and supplication in the Spirit, and watching thereunto with all perseverance and supplication for all saints. (Eph. 6:18)

Prayer is the work, and prayer works! So pray, then pray some more!

He Changed Me

———— 🦌 ————

Before I asked Jesus into my heart and entered into a love relationship with Him, I was tricked and deceived by the lies of the devil. First, I thought I had plenty of time to get ready. Even though years before, the Lord had shown me that there isn't always time. In the mid-1980s I was in a terrible car accident. Before the wreck, I thought if I were ever in danger I would just call upon the Lord. However, He was not on my mind when my car collided with another at seventy miles per hour. My last word before impact, which could have been the last word I ever spoke, was . . . You fill in the blank—it was not *shoot*.

Can you imagine facing Jesus and Him reminding you of your last word on earth? The accident had happened too quickly to call upon His name. So if you aren't in a love relationship with the King, reborn by the blood of the Lamb, you may not have time either.

Another deceiving trick that I fell for was believing I had to change my life, clean up my ways, before Jesus would want me. There was no way for me to change me. That is the Father, Son, and Holy Spirit's job. Once Jesus comes into your heart, He creates a will inside you that makes you want to do right. Through the power of the Holy Spirit, He then molds and makes you into a new creature. He gives you strength and power to change. "I can do all things through Christ which strengtheneth me" (Phil. 4:13).

The Holy Spirit revealed some things to me about myself and they were not pretty. He showed me how self-centered I had always been. This revelation came to me in the poem "I Want." (I sometimes wonder if I get rebukes on paper because I have always been so hard headed.)

I Want

How many times have I
Said, "I want"
I can't count the times
I do, but I can count the times I don't.
I've lived a self-centered life
All for me.
What I could do or have or
Want to see.
I never thought what God
Wanted to do through me,
Or how I should deny self
And serve Thee.
A God-centered life never
Entered my mind,
But I thought I was a good
Person true and kind.
I've been doing my own thing
And serving God when I had time.
I've always said I am too busy,
But I've been so blind.
Lord, forgive my self-centered ways
I promise to be God-centered for

The rest of my days.
I will serve You and wait for
Your commands.
Please Lord include me in all
Of Your plans.

As I reflected on my self-centeredness, I realized how tolerant and patient God had been with me, even through all my broken promises. I prayed this prayer that I call "Surrender All," and daily I realize I must surrender all.

SURRENDER ALL

Dear Lord, how many times have
I hurt You by promises I
Didn't keep?
How many times, Lord, did I
Make You weep?
Only You know, Lord, the times You've
Forgiven me of sin
For me to turn around and do
It all over again.
Lord, You are so patient and
Tolerant of me.
And now my time has come
To surrender all to Thee.
I will adjust my life and
Be obedient to Your call.
Lord, I give You my life.
I surrender all.
Amen.

The emptiness and unrest I once felt disappeared when Jesus came into my life. When He came, He brought—

PEACE

I found peace
I used to be so restless all
Day and night,
Something was missing, something
Was not right.
I never felt satisfied, I never felt content.
These feeling I couldn't change or
Even try to prevent.
But the day I confessed my sins
And those sins I repent
My days became filled with peace.
My life was content.
Our Lord saved me
And now I rejoice!
He is my Savior!
He is my choice!
Praise the Lord! Praise the Lord!

Thou wilt keep him in perfect peace, whose mind is stayed on thee. (Isa. 26:3)

Peace I leave with you, my peace I give unto you: not as the world giveth, give I unto you. (John 14:27)

And the peace of God, which passeth all understanding, shall keep your hearts and minds through Christ Jesus. (Phil. 4:7)

Only God can change us. We need only to surrender to Him, trust Him and allow His peace.

THE FULL ARMOR OF GOD

———— ❧ ————

One night I was studying in the book of Ephesians. Having never read the Bible prior to the few months before I was saved, I knew nothing about the full armor of God. The Holy Spirit brought this scripture to life and poured a poem through my pen.

THE FULL ARMOR OF GOD

Every morning I worship before
I begin my day.
I put on my full armor of God,
To defeat the devil's evil way.
I begin with the belt of truth
Wrapped around my waist.
With the breastplate of righteousness
Securely in place.
My feet firmly fitted with readiness,
That comes from the gospel of peace.
So temptation and unrest will
Surely cease.
Next is my shield of faith, to extinguish

The flaming arrows of the evil one.
But my armor is not complete,
My work is not done,
Until I put on the helmet of salvation
And hold the sword of the Spirit.
Now I am suited in the full armor
Of God and the devil can't come near it.
So, Satan, don't waste your time
On me!
God is my armor and He
Commands you to flee!

As I visualized putting on the full armor of God, I saw Jesus wrapping the belt of truth around my waist. Jesus is the truth, the way, and the life, and His Word tells us the truth will set us free. Jesus is my righteousness and the breastplate covers my heart, where Jesus lives. My feet are shod in the Word of God, firmly planted on the solid foundation, being prepared through His Word to be always ready. My faith is in Jesus. As I think about the shield of faith, I picture Jesus standing in front of me, protecting me from every arrow the enemy shoots. Jesus is my salvation, and He covers my head in the day of battle. The helmet of salvation protects my mind with the mind of Christ and with the soundness of mind that He promises. The only weapon in the armor is the sword—the powerful, heart-piercing Word of God.

Now that you are suited in the full armor of God, "Be strong in the Lord, and in the power of his might" (Eph. 6:10). Don't forget to put on your spiritual clothes today!

New Creature

The Lord began a quick work in my life from the moment I was saved. He gave me a hunger for His Word and an awesome desire to pray for hours. I would wake up early and stay up until the wee hours of the morning to commune with Him. I, truly, went on His enduring strength without getting weary. He brought insight and revelation into His Word each time I opened the Bible. He answered my prayers so quickly it was amazing. He knew I would be diagnosed with cancer twelve hours after I accepted Him as my Savior, and He was preparing me for the battle. I was His baby, and He cared for me as a good parent. I felt like a toddler taking my first step. God cheered me on, saying, "That's My girl." I knew I had the whole cheering squad in Heaven rooting for me. I was a brand-new girl with a new heart and spiritual eyes.

REBORN

The day I was reborn I entered
A whole new world.
I was given a new heart, soul, mind

And eyes. I am a brand-new girl.
My heart now swells with love for
The Lord and all His creations.
My soul cries out to Him, rejoicing and
Praising with unlimited expectations.
My mind is focused on Him to
Direct my footsteps and show me the way.
My sight is now through spiritual eyes
That see the blessing in every day.
I am alive, and Christ is
Alive in me.
I want to glorify Him for the
Whole world to see.

My understanding of success changed from the temporary to the eternal.

Charge them that are rich in this world, that they be not
high-minded, nor trust in uncertain riches, but in the
living God, who giveth us richly all things to enjoy; . . .
that they be rich in good works, ready to distribute, willing to communicate; Laying up in store for themselves a
good foundation against the time to come, that they may
lay hold on eternal life. (1 Tim. 6:17–19)

SPIRITUAL EYES

Thank you, Lord, for spiritual
Eyes.
You changed the way I look
At lives.
I used to think success meant

A title or money in the bank,
And people were important according
To their social rank.
I thought an expensive car and
A beautiful home
Symbolized wealth and success
Alone.
Oh, Lord, I now see through
Spiritual eyes,
And now know the treasures
Found in lives.
Success is salvation, living
In Christ.
Our treasures are in Heaven, because
Jesus paid the price.

"For where your treasure is, there will your heart be also" (Matt. 6:21). Everything in this lifetime—health, wealth, loved ones—can vanished forever, but eternal treasures last for eternity. Recognize the true meaning of success and store your treasures in Heaven.

Take Time to Think, God is the Power

Take time to think about God,
He is the power.
How much time do you give Him
A day, more than an hour?
He deserves every thought, every
Moment of everyday.
He created us for His purpose,
To live His way.
For our life to Him belongs.
Lift up words of praise, love
And songs.

Finally, brethren, whatsoever things are true, whatsoever things are honest, whatsoever things are just, whatsoever things are pure, whatsoever things are lovely, whatsoever things are of good report; if there be any virtue, and if there be any praise, think on these things. (Phil. 4:8)

Speaking to yourselves in psalms and hymns and spiritual songs, singing and making melody in your heart to the Lord. (Eph. 5:19)

We are new creations when Christ comes into our hearts, and He desires and deserves our constant, continuous devotion. We are created for His good pleasure and glory.

A STRANGER

Have you ever seen a
Stranger in need,
But you were too busy to
Do a good deed?
Have you ever passed a
Stranger by and
He stayed on your mind but
You didn't know why?
Has a stranger ever smiled or
Waved at you,
For you to turn your head
And wonder who and think
They must have mistaken you?
The next time you see a
Stranger in distress,
Think about our Lord, could
This be a test?
Who could this stranger be?
Could it be an angel
The Lord has sent to me?

Be not forgetful to entertain strangers: for thereby some have entertained angels unawares. (Heb. 13:2)

The day after the Lord inspired this poem, my husband was driving home from another state. He said he was singing praises to the Lord when a certain type of tire lug wrench came to mind. He thought this was strange, considering at the time his mind wasn't on tires. He said the impression of this tool became stronger and stronger; for miles that was all he could think of. As he came around a curve, he saw a car stranded on the side of the road and he stopped. Standing beside the car was a young couple with a newborn baby. The young man greeted my husband with a big smile and thanked him for stopping. He said they had been on the side of the road for over two hours, and numerous cars had passed by without anyone offering help. The closest house or phone was twenty miles away. Then, the young man asked my husband if he had that certain type of lug wrench. Together they changed two tires, and my husband witnessed to them, telling how the Lord had impressed him miles down the road about that tool. The young couple were new Christians, and they got so excited about how the Lord had sent them a Christian to help with the right tool!

When my husband came in that night he said, "I entertained strangers today that may have been angels."

The Bible teaches us a lot about angels. They are God's messengers, who have strength and wisdom; they are assigned to each child of God. They minister and protect the well-being of Gods' children.

In 1 Kings 19:4–7, God sent an angel to encourage Elijah. God sent an angel to protect Daniel in the lions' den in Daniel 6:22. Peter was delivered out of prison by an angel of the Lord in Acts 12:8–11.

My son Reid has a special Christmas story of how God sent an angel to protect him and delivered him from harm. Christmas day 1986, Santa Claus brought Reid a go-cart. He was riding it from our home to his grandparents' home and had to cross a fairly busy road. He turned too quickly and the go-cart flipped over, pinning him beneath. He was lying in the middle of the road with gasoline pouring all over him, and he could hear a car coming. He said he prayed for God to help. He knew that the car approaching around the curve would not be able to see him. When Reid opened his eyes, he saw a white truck pulling off the side of the road, and a big man, over six foot tall, got out. With one hand the man lifted up the go-cart and placed it in the yard. He then picked up Reid and told him, "You are fine." The man left without another word. Reid said he had never seen the truck or the man before, but the man's gentle way calmed him down, and he knew everything was OK. In a matter of seconds after the man left, a car came flying around the curve. Reid knew his life had been spared through divine intervention. I praise the Lord for protection.

> For he shall give his angels charge over thee, to keep thee in all thy ways. (Ps. 91:11)

> The angel of the Lord encampeth round about them that fear him, and delivereth them. (Ps. 34:7)

We may be unaware when angels watch over us or when we entertain them, but we have God's word that both take place. Be kind to everyone and always have a spirit of thanksgiving.

The Mighty Little Weapon

The dictionary defines the tongue as the act or power of speaking; a moveable muscular structure attached to the floor of the mouth. In the Bible, the tongue is described as a little thing that can cause great harm. The tongue can be as a flame setting fire, or wickedness and poison to the body. We are instructed to bridle our tongue, to control it. I must confess I used to use my tongue in full force, and I could lash out and cut sharper than a razor. Well, the Lord revealed to me how I had used this little member in a big way. It was my weapon and I kept it loaded, ready to fire.

THINK FIRST, NOT TONGUE FIRST

Our tongue is our weapon, we
use it with full force.
It doesn't need to be reloaded, it
takes a natural course.
We aim at our target and shoot
Straight ahead.
Without the worry of what is
Being said.

If only we would think before
We say.
For God's perfect will, His purpose
And His perfect way.
Our weapon could be turned friendly
And offer comfort and peace.
Our warfare of tongues would
Completely cease.
Think of God first in all you do,
And use your tongue for praise
And words true.

If any man among you seem to be religious, and bridleth not his tongue, but deceiveth his own heart, this man's religion is vain. (James 1:26)

Even so the tongue is a little member, and boasteth great things. Behold, how great a matter a little fire kindleth! And the tongue is a fire, a world of iniquity: so is the tongue among our members, that it defileth the whole body, and setteth on fire the course of nature; and it is set on fire of hell. . . . But the tongue can no man tame it; it is an unruly evil, full of deadly poison. (James 3:5–6, 8)

Many times I tried, and for many years my New Year's resolutions involved trying to control my tongue. These resolutions were soon broken because of the root of the problem: me! I couldn't change me, but Jesus changed me. Now, He controls my tongue. I praise God for that, and believe me, a lot of wounded people do too. Once Jesus is inside of you, He will make you think first not tongue first.

SMILE

The one thing that everyone has to give away freely is a smile, and usually when one is given one is received. I have been amazed at how many unhappy Christians are in churches today. So many have forgotten to tell their face they are saved.

> Blessed is the people that know the joyful sound: they shall walk, O Lord, in the light of thy countenance. In thy name shall they rejoice all the day. (Ps. 89:15–16)

CHRISTIAN STYLE

What is your Christian style?
Do you wear a frown or do
You share a smile?
Christians should be happy, we
Should always wear a smile.
Our dress should be the full armor
Of God, joy is our style.
We should light up a room when
We walk in.

Sharing God's love and praising
Him.
It could be contagious, it could
Really catch on.
Others will want to be happy,
They will want to belong.
To the family of Christians
With a joyful style
Living for the Lord, always
Wearing a smile.

As believers, we are being observed by unbelievers. They watch as we endure trials and pressure to see if we bend under them or soar above them, with a happy countenance. Let others see the joy of the Lord on your face no matter the circumstances, because we cannot only tell our problems to Jesus, we can speak the power of Jesus to our problems.

If you are saved
And you know it
Give a smile!
If you are saved
And you know it
Give a smile!
If you are saved
And you know it,
Then let your face show it!
If you are saved
And you know it
Give a smile!

GOD'S TIMING

In October 1993, I had a very successful hysterectomy and all the cancer in the cervix was removed. The operation margins were clear, so I did not have to take chemotherapy treatments. The doctors found nodular tumors in my lymph nodes, so they removed them as well. After several pathology readings, the findings remained unresolved. The slides were sent to another state for further review. Then, on January 4, 1994, I received a call from my doctor with a bad report—malignant non-Hodgkin lymphoma.

I had a previous operation in 1991 to remove some tumors in my neck, but all those reports had come back unresolved. Now, these were reevaluated, and diagnosed as positive for cancer. I had gone to doctors for about three years because of the lumps, and everyone seemed unconcerned. The doctors had said if they were cancer I would be dead by now. Through all the wrong diagnoses I can see God's grace and mercy; He knew I could not battle cancer without Him. Quite frankly I would have given up and died.

This time the word *cancer* didn't frighten me as much as before. I almost felt relief to know what was wrong with me, but I made a terrible mistake. I took my life back into my own control without praying about what God wanted me to do. Everything went wrong; God tried to shut doors and I forced my way through them.

First, the doctor I was scheduled to see had an emergency surgery the day of my appointment, so I insisted on seeing his associate. That was the first door I pushed open, and from there it got worst. We did not start off with a good patient-doctor relationship. The day I had to have a bilateral bone biopsy and marrow aspiration, the doctor had run out of the drugs normally used for sedation. Needless to say, that was the most excruciating procedure I've ever experienced. I curled into a fetal position and cried for six hours. The next day, I was black and blue from the bruises and could barely walk. Then I received a telephone call— the bone and marrow were frozen before it got to the testing laboratory in another state and they wanted another biopsy. I said, "No! No! No!"

I got down on my knees, crying out to God. I could not understand why He allowed this to happen to me. He softly comforted me and reminded me how I forced my way through every door He shut. Then He gave me this poem, "God's Timing."

GOD'S TIMING

God, Your timing is perfect,
Only You are perfect and good.
Sometimes we aren't patient and we
Don't do the things we should.
We get frustrated and can't
Understand why,
But if we would slow down,

We would see You standing by.
We get in a hurry and want
Things done now.
And don't take time to wait for
The things You allow.
Please grant me patience, Lord,
To listen to Your voice,
For Your perfect timing, Your
Will I shall rejoice!

For my thoughts are not your thoughts, neither are my ways your ways, saith the Lord. For as the heavens are higher than the earth, so are my ways higher than your ways, and my thoughts than your thoughts. (Isa. 55:8–9)

Sometimes a shut door is an answer. When this happens, seek God's direction; ask Him to show you the door of opportunity; and ask Him to lead you through. Be confident a prayer is never answered late. God is absolutely on time.

SEEKING THE LORD

———— 🕊 ————

I was very confused after my first experience of shut doors. I didn't know where to go for medical help, but I certainly knew where to go for guidance and direction—to the Lord in prayer. I stormed Heaven for two weeks before I felt any direction. During this time, I went through a lot of emotions. The doctor had said my time was limited and I needed urgent care.

So this poem is about feeling blue.

BLUE

Sometimes you feel down
And blue.
You feel the whole world
Is against you, too.
You feel lost and sad
Inside,
But always remember who
Is at your side.
Our Lord walks with you
Everyday.

So keep Him in your thoughts
And every word you say
Always remember our Lord
Loves you
And that He hears your sorrows
And cries with you, too.

The Lord answered my prayers, and when I felt led to
call Mayo Clinic, a Christian answered the phone. Immediately, doors began to fly open. God is so good!

We grow through pain even though it is not pleasant.
Our experiences work like fertilizer that God uses to help
us mature and grow strong. God sends the proper nutrition
we need.

GOD ANSWERS

———— 🌿 ————

G od provided **every way** for me to get to Mayo Clinic; I knew this was an answered prayer. I truly liked the oncologist and all the staff, but one big obstacle was thrown in my path. The doctor wanted to do a bone and marrow biopsy. I was frightened beyond words. The nightmare of the previous one was too fresh in my memory. As I sat in the waiting room and wept over the procedure that had to be done, a beautiful woman came up to me and asked if I was all right. I immediately told her, "No! I'm scared to death. The doctors say I must have a bone marrow biopsy, and I can't do it again. I'll just go home." She told me to go over to the motel, and she would see what she could do. When Avery, my husband, and I got to the motel, I was ready to pack up and go home. He gently but firmly reminded me that God had opened every door and we had to see this through. I called home and pleaded for prayer chains to get started. My prayer partner, Cindi, said, "You need a miracle and we will ask God for one." When I hung up, I went into the bathroom and got on my knees. This was my prayer.

Dear God, I need a miracle! This procedure may not be anything to some of your children but it is to me. I can't do this God; I'm scared. You promise in Your Word that You will not put more on us than we can stand, and Lord I can't stand this. You promise to make a way of escape, and I need a way out. Help me! Give me a miracle. Amen.

By this time, Avery is knocking on the bathroom door saying it is time to go to the clinic. I reluctantly opened the door and headed back to the clinic. I cannot tell you I did it with peace in my heart or that I was no longer frightened, because I was trembling. When we got to the doctor's office, the woman who had approached me earlier came up to me and said, "Mrs. Beard, you've got a miracle! You are going to be the first person at Mayo to be put to sleep for this procedure. God gave you your miracle!"

GOD ANSWERS

When you face trials and suffering
And have no ability to deal
know in your heart God has the
Answer and wait for Him to reveal.
Be of good courage and let God protect.
Remember you are His chosen, His select.
He has a plan for your life, pray for His will.
Then be fruitful and patient, trust and be still.

God is the answer and He does answer. I am so thankful He responds quickly when the need is urgent. Do you have an urgent need in your life? Do you need a way of escape? If so, call upon Him who promises not to put more on you than you can bear, and ask Him for a way of escape.

> There hath no temptation [test or trial] taken you but such as is common to man: but God is faithful, who will not suffer you to be tempted above that ye are able; but will with the temptation also make the way to escape, that ye may be able to bear it. (1 Cor. 10:13)

I received a miracle, and I recognize it as one. I praise God, for He is still in the miracle-working business.

MIRACLES

> Miracles happen every single day.
> Do you believe they come your way?
> Do you have faith when you lift up
> Your prayer?
> Can you feel how much God truly cares?
> Miracles come packaged big and small.
> But a miracle is a miracle through it all.
> Some we must have spiritual eyes to see
> And others are as obvious as can be.
> Miracles do happen every single day!

Believe a miracle is on its way!!!

We have God's promise that all things are possible—not some or one but *all*. Pray His word to Him for the need in your life. "With God all things are possible" (Mark 10:27). Believe His promise, have faith that nothing is impossible or too difficult for God. "All things are possible to him that believeth" (Mark 9:23).

Father,

I know that You are aware of my circumstance and that You are in total control of everything that touches my life. My trust is in You. My hope is in You, and I lift up this prayer in faith believing all things are possible with You. I thank You and praise You for who You are and all You do. In Your Son's holy name, Jesus, my Lord and Savior. Amen.

He Prepared Me

Have you ever had a dream where you felt the Lord was speaking to you, giving you a message? The very first time this happened to me was in February 1994, when I was awaiting the results of the diagnostic test and pathology reports for a complete diagnosis and prognosis.

The message was to prepare me for the days ahead, and it consisted of three dreams. In the first dream, I was in a large room and suddenly the room became crowded. People were everywhere shouting and crying; there was total confusion. I began crying out to the Lord for a door to get out. Immediately, I found a door and entered into another large room. It wasn't long before the room became crowded again with turmoil and confusion. Once again, I cried out to the Lord for a door, and again, He provided. The same thing happened a third time. This time I pleaded in a desperate cry, and I found a door. When I opened the door, I saw green pastures and a cool breeze blew upon my face.

I awoke with the feeling of peace and the presence of God. I went back to sleep and began to dream I was in a winding hallway almost like a maze. It was dark with only a little light shining from the distance. I began to follow the light. When I found the source, it was a small round window with what looked like a blind on it. Farther down the hallway I saw another light. I continued on to a larger window. I journeyed from large window to larger until finally I saw a light that was as big as the hallway and too bright to look at. As I stood there, I felt heat against my face and warmth surge through my body.

Once again, I awoke with the feeling that I was in the presence of the Lord, God Almighty. As His peace flooded my soul, I fell back to sleep, entering into the last dream. I saw a large boat with a man dressed in festive attire motioning for me to come aboard. When I boarded the ship, a flock of people began filing in. As I sat on a tiny seat, the water became very rough, with angry waves beating against the boat. The passengers became very upset and were crying and shouting. I sat there and said, "Lord, they need to be still." The more they shouted the larger the waves became. The water rushed over the boat and the passengers were swept into the sea. I continued to say, "Lord, they need to be still!" Instantly, I was in a small canoe floating down a crystal-clear river with green grass and trees on both sides. A cool, refreshing breeze blew my hair as the words *peace, be still* echoed in the stillness.

When I awoke, I immediately got out of bed and went to my knees in prayer, then to search the Word of God for understanding. The Holy Spirit revealed to me that Jesus is the door, He is the Everlasting Light and He is my peace.

> I am the door: by me if any man enter in, he shall be saved, and shall go in and out, and find pasture. (John 10:9)

The Lord shall be unto thee an everlasting light, and thy God thy glory. (Isa. 60:19)

God is our refuge and strength, a very present help in trouble. Therefore will not we fear, though the earth be removed, and though the mountains be carried into the midst of the sea; Though the waters thereof roar and be troubled, though the mountains shake with the swelling thereof. . . . There is a river, the streams whereof shall make glad the city of God, the holy place of the tabernacles of the most High. God is in the midst of her; she shall not be moved: God shall help her, and that right early. . . . Be still, and know that I am God. (Ps. 46:1–5,10).

HE GAVE ME THREE DREAMS

In three dreams the Lord prepared me for
Some unknown struggles I was about to face.
The first dream He showed me He would
Provide a door to always open in the right place.
The second dream He showed me He was my
Everlasting light.
That He would direct my path to be just and
right.
The third and final dream He provided me with
Perfect peace.
He told me to be still and patient and my troubles
Would surely cease.
Weeks after these dreams confusion and trouble
Came upon me,
But He also opened doors for me to see.
His everlasting light showed me the way.

And through Him perfect peace filled my day.
As long as I keep my eyes on Him and trust and believe
He will always open doors, His everlasting light will
Guide my way and His perfect peace I will receive.

A week or so after these dreams, I received a diagnosis of stage-four lymphoma, with metastasis to the bone marrow. The prognosis was grave, with little encouragement of remission and none of a cure. This news brought fear to my family with a host of emotions, including the turmoil and confusion that I had dreamed about. However, I knew the Lord had prepared me for this battle, and I had His word, His promise, that He would provide doors, guidance, and peace. As I faced the beginning of chemotherapy with little hope from the world, I focused on the only hope, Jesus Christ.

No matter what you may be facing in your life today *Jesus* is your hope, your answer, and your peace. He will prepare you for the battle. He will sustain you in every crisis. He will guide you through each situation and carry you to victory.

You Are More Valuable than Many Little Sparrows

When I took my first chemo treatment, I was told I would lose my hair in seven to seventeen days. I felt overwhelmed by panic. I had always thought my long blond hair was the best outward feature I had, and now that would be gone. I was also told that I would gain weight due to the prednisone intake. I thought, *Oh, no—not fat and bald!*

A few days after the worst side effects of the treatment had subsided, I went on a wig hunt with Cindi, my prayer partner, who, fortunately, was my hairdresser, too. This experience was worse than we had imagined. Everything I tried on looked like a wig; nothing looked natural, and certainly not like my own hair. At the last shop we went into, I saw a wig in a magazine that looked very similar to my hair, the same color and cut. The shop's owner said she would order it, but I would have to pay for it first and there was a no return, no refund policy. I wasn't about to pay several hundreds of dollars for something I couldn't even try on, so Cindi and I left with no wig and much discouragement. The ride home was silent. What can someone say at that point? In the stillness of that moment, I prayed,

"Lord, if You don't want me to have a wig, then give me peace, and help me be content in this situation."

That night my sister Sandra called. She was going shopping the next day in a much larger city, and she offered to look for a wig for me. To my surprise, she called me back and described a wig that resembled the one in the magazine. So I went off on another wig hunt. At the wig shop I couldn't believe my eyes; there it was, my wig! I shouted, "That's the wig I wanted!" The woman in the shop said, "Well, honey, I don't know how it got here. I didn't order it. A UPS man who I've never seen before brought it in yesterday, one hour before your sister came in." I knew how it got there: My God, Jehovah Jireh, provided that wig. It was perfect in color, style, and fit!

I was excited to have the wig, but I was still anxious about my hair loss. Daily, I would see strands of long blond hair on my pillow, in the shower, and on the floor as a constant reminder that baldness was steadily approaching. One day, as I sat in the den crying out to the Lord about how frightened and ashamed I felt over my hair loss, I noticed a sparrow holding onto the screen of the window. A few minutes later several more came to the window. When I went into the kitchen, sparrows were on the screen of the window there, too. In each room that I went into, sparrows were looking in the windows. This was very unusual. I had lived in this home over ten years and never before had I seen this happened. Then I sensed the presence of the Lord, and I knew He was speaking to me through these little birds.

After several days of searching the scriptures and praying for the Holy Spirit to reveal the meaning of the sparrows, the Lord led me late one night to Matthew 10:29–31.

Are not two sparrows sold for a farthing? And one of them shall not fall on the ground without your Father. But the very hairs of your head are all numbered. Fear not therefore, ye are of more value than many sparrows.

There was my answer. I was so excited I shouted and just about woke up the entire household.

This was a difficult time in my life, and God let me know He cared, even about the number of hairs on my head. He is no respecter of person, and He cares for you. He knows the very number of hairs on your head, no matter how many or how few. In His Word He doesn't speak of the beautiful red bird or the brilliant blue bird but of the common little sparrow, plentiful in number and one hardly noticed. He even knows the number of tears you've shed, (Ps. 56:8). He cares about *you*!

God cares so much about His children, and He supplies all of their needs according to His riches in glory by Christ Jesus (Phil. 4:19). The wig that God provided me was never intended for my use; God had other plans. One night while I was attending a revival, a beautiful young woman with long blond hair went forward for prayer. At that moment the Holy Spirit spoke to me and told me to give her my wig. As I sat there I struggled with that prompting, thinking *I might need that wig, my hair is falling out.* I even said in my mind, "But, Lord, You gave me that wig." Over and over in my mind, the prompting continued. By the end of the service, I was convinced I had to give her my wig, even though it appeared she had hair. It was one of those things you don't understand, you just do.

I didn't know her name or how to get in touch with her, so I told a friend about what the Lord said I had to do. God began networking people to get the message to her. About three weeks later, she called me. By this time, at least one-third of my hair was gone, leaving bald spots throughout. She said, "Hi, Cindy! I hear you have a wig you want to give away. This is my answer to prayer. I've been bald since I was two years old. I have been praying for a new wig for three months, because I didn't have the money to buy one. This is my miracle." I listened as sweet tears of joy rolled down my face and the fragrance of Jesus filled the air. I could barely speak without crying. I knew I was witnessing the hand of God providing for His children's needs. I shared with her how God had handpicked her wig, when I thought the entire time it was for me.

We immediately bonded that special day, and God blessed me with a new sister in Christ Jesus. But that wasn't the only blessing God gave because of obedience. Within a few days after giving her the wig, I noticed the bald spots had new hair growth. Every time hair fell out, God replaced it with new hair. I never needed a wig! God is so good. His ways and thoughts are so much higher and better than we could ever think or imagine.

There is no way to out give God; He owns it all. He tells us in Luke 6:38 to "Give, and it shall be given unto you; good measure, pressed down, and shaken together, and running over." He wants to bless you, and He takes pleasure in giving to His children. "God loveth a cheerful giver" (2 Cor. 9:7). There are joy and blessings in giving, because, "It is more blessed to give than to receive" (Acts 20:35). He cares for every little sparrow and knows all of their needs. Remember *you* are more valuable than many sparrows, so tell Him what you need. "Ask, and it shall be given you" (Luke 11:9). You never know when God might use you to be an instrument of blessing to others, or others may be used to bless you.

Household Salvation

In 1991, my son, Reid, and daughter, Shawn, ages twelve and ten asked Jesus into their hearts and were baptized. They attended church regularly and participated in many church activities, but neither seemed to have a passion for Jesus. As time passed, I felt a burden in my heart that they may be growing cold. During this time, I was in my second battle with cancer, taking high-dose chemotherapy. I needed assurance that they knew Jesus personally.

One beautiful spring day, as I looked around, I saw new life. The grass looked like emeralds sparkling in the sun. The dogwood trees were in full bloom, dancing in the breeze. The azaleas looked liked they had all been hand painted by the Master. Every living thing was full of God's glory, exclaiming His splendor. I said, "Lord, I want my children to be instruments of Your glory, to come alive in You." Instantly, the Holy Spirit inspired this prayer for my children.

Save My Children

Lord, save my children, I cry
Out to You each night.
I pray they give their lives

To You and keep You
In their sight.
I pray they know You, Jesus, and
The love You freely give.
I pray they find salvation
So they can truly live.
Lord save my children.
I surrender them to You.
Lord, hear my cries, as I trust
And believe You do.
Amen.

Within a few months, I witnessed a rebirth in both of my kids. Reid was fifteen and Shawn thirteen when the spark kindled into a flame. They both had been at a youth revival and the power of God touched their hearts in a life-changing way.

I was in my prayer closet, storming Heaven on their behalf, when I heard *tap, tap, tap* on the door. It was Shawn. She asked if she could come in and pray with me. With tears falling down her sweet little face, she told me about her encounter with Jesus at the altar. She described in glorious detail her total rededication to her Lord. As I embraced her, we wept with tears of joy and shouts of praises to the King of Kings. Then Reid told me about the anointed saxophone player whose music touched his heart and moved him to his knees trembling in the presence of God.

This mother's prayers had been answered by the touch of the Master's hand on the hearts of her heartstrings.

Do you have a loved one who is lost or who has grown cold to the love of Jesus? If so pray, pray, *and* pray, some more. Your prayers are like launching a rocket that hits its target every time. God will pierce their hearts when we use the weapon of prayer.

Young Men Shall See Visions, Old Men Shall Dream Dreams

God will turn every test into a testimony and every trial into a blessing. In Romans 8:28, we read, "And we know that all things work together for good to them that love God, to them who are called according to his purpose."

During my battles with cancer, God has proved Himself over and over in my life. So much good has come from every affliction. One of the most awesome events was the change not only in my immediate family but also in the lives of my parents, granddaddy, sisters, and their families.

My granddaddy, at the golden age of eighty, asked Jesus into his heart. One day he told me, "Cindy, you need to know me and the Lord are best friends." He said he had to give his heart to Jesus so his prayers for my healing would be heard. He also wanted all his family to be reunited in Heaven someday. Immediately, I was taken back to the hours I spent on my knees in prayer for his salvation. Then he shared with me the dream God had given him.

PAPA'S DREAM

My grandfather dreamed the Lord
Had a mission for him to do.
To get people to heaven, so he
Thought it carefully through.
He decided to rent a plane large
Enough to hold everyone.
But he counted his money and he
Knew it couldn't be done.
Then from heaven he heard a
Loud voice say,
"You get them ready and I'll
Provide the way."

My granddaddy is a powerful prayer warrior today, continuously interceding on the behalf of others. He is a bold witness for Jesus. His ordained mission is to get everyone ready to meet Jesus.

My daddy says that He was plucked out of the fire by the hand of the Savior. Now he is on fire for the Lord and has a passion for the lost. The Lord gave him a vision of people being tricked by the devil into believing they could be good enough to go to heaven.

THREE BUSES

The Lord showed my daddy
a vision of three buses on a road.
The first bus was heaven bound
with a spirit-filled load.
The second bus's destination was

A one-way trip to hell.
But the third bus was a trick of
The devil, a lie he loves to tell.
The passengers thought they were
Going to heaven but they were
On their way to hell.
The Lord said, there are only two
Buses, the choice is yours to choose.
Either you accept Christ as your Savior
Or you're lost and you lose.

My entire family now puts Jesus first in all they do. Maybe it took the life-threatening illness of a loved one to see God's love more clearly. Only God knows that answer, but I've seen the life-changing results of *all* things working for the good of those who love the Lord. I am seeing in my own life that, "It shall come to pass in the last days, saith God, I will pour out of my Spirit upon all flesh: and your sons and your daughters shall prophesy, and your young men shall see visions, and your old men shall dream dreams" (Acts 2:17).

There is a purpose for everything, a reason for every season in your life. God may be using you and the struggles in your life to bring someone into the Kingdom of God. There is no way to know all who are watching you walk through the fire or your journey through the valley, but be assured, if God has allowed it, then there is a purpose. So claim His promise that all will work together for good. Ask Him to reveal these truths to you and expect to see His mighty power work in your life and in the lives of others.

GOD PLANNED IT ALL

When God calls us to do something, He works out everything, and everything has a purpose. I experienced this firsthand on an out-of-state speaking engagement. When I was invited to go to a church four-and-a-half hours away from home, I went to the Lord in prayer to seek His direction and wisdom concerning who was to travel with me. Normally that wouldn't be an issue because my husband would go, but this time he was out of town due to his job. During my prayer time, a friend came to mind, but we had never gone anywhere together before. I couldn't imagine why I was to ask her, so I asked of the Lord again. Once again, He directed me to ask her. I immediately called her, and she gladly accepted the invitation to go.

As we left on this journey, I still wondered why God had led me to ask her. I knew she was a prayer warrior, so I assumed that had to be it. However, He had much more in store than that. We had traveled over four hours and were soon to arrive at our destination when she asked me the pastor's name. When I told her the pastor's and his wife's names, my friend was shocked. She began sharing about her childhood and how, when they were children, this pastor's wife had picked on her to the point of being cruel.

I was amazed at how God had arranged this unexpected reunion. God didn't allow her to ask their names until we were almost there. To think, some forty years had passed since they had last spoken. This was *big* and it was getting bigger. When we arrived at the accommodations the church had arranged, I was surprised to see that they had chosen such a poorly kept place. It appeared to be an hourly motel where only the roaches checked in. It did not look safe or clean and definitely not a place where I would stay.

I didn't know what to do; I didn't want to offend the people who had invited me. After my friend and I discussed it briefly, we decided I should get the key and hope for the best. The desk clerk gave me the key and instructions to get in the room quickly, lock the doors, and not go out unnecessarily. When we drove around to our room, the people next door were partying outside, and the "working girls" were making their rounds. As we sat in front of the room in our locked car expressing our disappointment, I heard a stern voice speak: *Foxes have holes and birds of the air have nest, but the Son of man has nowhere to lay His head.* My heart broke and tears began to flow down my cheeks. I knew I had disappointed my Lord with my grumbling and complaining. I repeated to my friend what the Holy Spirit had spoken to me. A holy hush fell as we very quickly got our things out of the car and headed to the door of our room. When we open it, we couldn't believe what we saw. The room was beautiful. It had fresh paint, new carpet, new furniture; it looked as if no one had ever stayed there before. We were amazed at what God had provided, but with His words still fresh on my heart, I don't think it would have mattered. My Savior didn't have anywhere to lay His head when He ministered.

That weekend old hurts were healed and forgiveness replaced resentment in my friend's life, and I learned a lesson on being humble.

Every person, every experience in life, serves a purpose in God's divine plan for our lives. We may not understand, but we can trust Him to prepare us for the journey that is ahead.

HOMECOMING

M any times as we travel to our destination, we pass strangers walking or hitchhiking. If you are like me you might pray a prayer of blessing and even entertain the thought of offering a ride, but the fear of what could happen keeps it just a thought of helping.

I was heading home from town one late spring evening as the sun was setting. I looked at my gas gauge and realized it was on empty, so I made a detour to the gas station. I looked over to my right and saw a young man walking along the side of the road. He was wearing a basketball shirt with a yellow number 22 on the back. I prayed a short prayer for him, and I sensed sadness in my spirit. About this time I had approached the gas station, and all the pumps were occupied. I circled the block, and when I returned, a space was opened. After pumping my gas, I went inside to write a check. I overheard Libby, the clerk, directing someone to pass right by my house, some six miles away. A young man's voice said, "Thank you, ma'am." When I looked up it was the young man who had been walking down the road, wearing the number 22.

When he left, I told Libby I felt as if the Lord was leading me to give him a ride. She warned me of the dangers of a woman picking up strangers, then said she would pray for me. I assured her I would do it only if I was sure it was of the Lord. Right before I got into my car, Libby gave me a window decal—John 3:16.

I immediately started praying, "Lord, show me if you want me to offer him a ride. Let me know beyond a shadow of a doubt. Show me, Lord." As I approached him he was walking with his back towards me. Suddenly, he jumped in front of my car, waving both arms and yelling. "Stop! Help me!"

As I slowed to a stop, I said, "OK, Lord, protect me." The young man ran up to the passenger window and said, "Thank you for stopping; I need help. I'm lost and it is almost dark. I don't know where I am or how to get to where I am going." He was dirty; he had long greasy hair and was unshaven. He wore filthy clothes and smelled awful.

I firmly said, "I need to know if you are going to harm me."

"No, ma'am," he replied.

"Well, before you get into my car, I need to know if I should be fearful of you."

"No, ma'am. I don't mean any harm; I just want a ride. I am trying to find my mama's house. I haven't seen her in twelve years."

This young man was desperate and afraid, so my last statement before he got into the car was, "Son, I feel the Lord sent me to help you. I am a Christian and Jesus is with me, so I am trusting you to behave. Get in."

He thanked me over and over when he got in and reassured me he meant no harm. His awful smell filled my car as we rode in silence, but quickly the silence was broken by some strange noises he began to make. I didn't know what was wrong, so I asked him if he was OK. He told he was frightened. Twelve years before, he had been taken away from his mother and put into foster care, and he had not seen or heard from her during that time. He hitchhiked ninety miles and found his grandmother's house, but she had passed away and the house had been sold. All afternoon he had walked around town asking if anyone knew his mother. Finally someone recognized her name and gave him directions to her house. He told me he was not familiar with the area and had no idea how to find it. I told him I had prayed for him when I first passed him. Then, when I overheard the directions he had been given at the gas station, I realized that he would be going exactly the way I was going. I told him Jesus loved him very much, and that God had placed me at the right place at the right time to provide him a ride. I asked him if he knew Jesus, and he said yes. I asked him if he was saved, and he said yes. I shared how Jesus had spared my life through battles of cancer, and he shared how Jesus had brought him through two heart attacks.

We passed by my house, and I told him we had only about one mile before he would be at his mother's house. He became very nervous. I asked him if I could pray for him. He thankfully said yes. As I began to pray, the Holy Spirit reminded me of the parable of the prodigal son. I prayed for his mother to greet him with open arms and welcome him back into the family. I prayed that he would be filled with love, peace, and joy. As soon as I said *amen*, we spotted the house that fit the description on the directions. A man was standing in the yard, so I told this lost son I would wait in the car to see if it was the right house. He thanked me for the ride and walked over to the man. I saw him nod yes, and the young man turned around and waved at me, but I couldn't pull out of the driveway until I saw the homecoming. The young man's mother came to the door and wrapped her arms around him.

Joy and thanksgiving filled my soul as I drove home. I had witness a child being returned to his mother after twelve years. When I walked into my house, I shared with my husband what had happened. Then the phone rang. It was Libby, from the store. She was calling to make sure I was home safe. She had been praying since I had left the store. God had covered all bases for this young man's homecoming and my safety, plus given me an incredible experience of His amazing love and grace.

In Luke 15:11–32, the parable of the lost son, we can feel the love God has for us. He is *always* watching, waiting, and longing for His child to return to Him, and He runs to meet us with a loving embrace. No matter if it is one day, one month, or many years we have been away, God is waiting for us to return to Him.

Faith

Faith is defined in Hebrews 11:1 as, "The substance of things hoped for, the evidence of things not seen." The dictionary defines faith as unquestionable belief, complete trust, and confidence. This is what we must have in order to please God—faith.

Faith goes beyond our human reasoning, soaring above the impossibilities and looking through eyes of hope focusing on the one hope, Jesus Christ. Faith is knowing that God is in total control of every situation and that He knows and gives what is best for His children.

Faith

Faith is given to everyone
In the same amount.
While some let it grow and flourish
And others kill it with doubt.

The ones who walk by faith
And practice it everyday,

Can see above the storms of life
And find peace along the way.

While others stay in confusion and turmoil,
They look for somebody to blame.
Wishing they had someone else's faith,
Never realizing they were given the same.

God has given every one of us the gift of faith. He tells us in Matthew 17:20, "If you have the faith as a grain of mustard seed, ye shall say unto this mountain, move from here to yonder place; and it shall move; and nothing shall be impossible unto you."

You have enough faith for anything God allows to come your way. If you could not endure it through Him, He wouldn't allow it. Remember, God knows everything about you. If you are given a test of faith, whether it be a pop quiz or a lengthy exam, rest assured He has prepared you for the test. He knows you are going to pass. You may not feel as if you are passing, but faith is not based on feelings, it is grounded with confidence in God. In Psalm 37:24, we have an awesome promise: "Though he fall, he shall not be utterly cast down: for the Lord upholdeth him with his hand." So if we trip or slip, God is reaching down to pick us up, brush us off, and breathe in us the strength to go forward.

So right now let's exercise. You do not even have to get up from your chair. Say with me:

Lord Jesus, I thank you that you are my hope. My confidence is not in me it is in you. In You alone, I place my trust and my faith. Help me to guard this precious gift of faith and to exercise it with every breath I take. I give you the burdens of today and ask you to be Lord over every situation in my life. I love you and praise you with all of my heart, soul, mind, and strength. Amen.

You are ready for whatever comes your way. You have the shield of faith, Jesus, in front of you and the power of the Holy Spirit inside of you. It's going to be a great day!

THE WAR WITHIN

Looking at the clouds of yesterday and the storms of tomorrow, I couldn't see the sun of today. Immediately, I was visited by Self who encouraged me to look at my past failures and uncertain futures. Self suggested I have a party and invite Pity who would bring along many companions. Before I realized what had happened, my house was shaken by a host of emotions. Anxious was the first to arrive, then Worry, Doubt, Fear, Sorrow, Pain, Weakness, and Discouragement all were there. They shouted unanimously and viciously until Despair came rushing in. He stood there laughing and ushered in Defeat.

In the darkness of turmoil and the midst of confusion, a soft voice began to powerfully speak, and the demons of defeat began to tremble with fear. "Be still My child, for the victory is near. Command the enemy of self to flee; call upon my help; look to Me. Take off the yoke of pity, put on the garment of praise. Lift up your head and raise your arms. I will make good what the enemy meant for harm. Lean on My everlasting arms."

Immediately Victory stepped in with a host of heavenly help. Praise destroyed Pity. Peace struck down Anxious. Faith demolished Worry, Doubt, and Fear. Comfort wiped out Sorrow and Pain. Strength overtook Weakness. Encouragement stomped out Discouragement. Despair and Defeat ran from Victory, and the Light of the world filled this girl. Praise was raised in thanksgiving and joy, in a loud shout! For there was no doubt, her warrior God had won the fight. Not a moment too late, His timing's right.

Words of wisdom are never to entertain self with pity; minister to Him with praise.

It is so easy to fall into the pit of self-pity. Every one of us has felt despair at some point in our lives. The times that I have been overcome by self-pity, I grabbed onto the rope of praise to pull, literally, myself out of the pit. When the praise to God is raised, He elevates us out of the pit. The sacrifice of praise is when you don't feel like praising, and when you don't feel like praising the Lord, you need to praise Him the most. Praise is a mighty weapon; the enemy cannot defeat a praising Christian. One powerful example of this is found in Acts 16. Paul and Silas were in prison, bound in chains. They sang praises to God, and He sent an earthquake to break the chains and set them free. Praise to God sets us free from the pit of pity. Victory is won through praise. Like the battle, recorded in 2 Chronicles 20:20–25, in which King Jehoshapt and his people praised the Lord and the enemy armies were destroyed.

Minister to the Lord of Lords and King of Kings, when the praises go up the blessings come down. Praise the Lord; again praise the Lord!

When you feel the demon of lies wants you to throw a pity party, sing this little chorus. Put your own tune to it and sing. The Holy Spirit gave this to me, and I walked around my house singing, stomping my feet, clapping my hands and won the war within. Remember Jesus has already won the battle, and we have the victory in the name of Jesus! Step on D's feet because he is defeated!

WIN THE WAR WITHIN

You demons of lies,
I call you by name,
I'm here to do battle,
Not play your game.
Run, fear, run!
Your day with me is done!
Victory has stepped in
And victory has won.
Go, doubt, go!
You've haunted me enough.
I'm praising my King and
I am sick of your stuff.
Flee, worry, flee!
You're through with worrying me.
I'm filled with peace and
Now you must cease.
Leave, pity, leave!
You can't deceive.
I am praising my King
And pity can't sing.
You're defeated, despair!
You can't discourage me.
For I am standing in
VICTORY!
Yes! My God is a warrior God
He commands a Heavenly Host.
He's my joy, and in Him I boast.
He's commander of His Heavenly Host.
He is chief and I am His child! I will not listen to
the enemy of lies!

THE ENCOURAGER

Every day we experience God in different ways, according to our needs. One of the daily encounters we can have with God is as our Encourager. He knows what we need and when we need it. He encourages us with love, peace, and joy through prayer, Bible study, other Christians, and circumstances He ordains.

We can read in Judges 6:12 how God encouraged Gideon when he was hiding in the winepress, feeling cowardly and frightened. God called him a "man of valor" or "mighty warrior." Talk about encouragement, Gideon was given God-confidence. God saw who he was going to be and greatly encouraged him.

Many times in my own life I knew God personally encouraged me. There were times when no one knew what I was going through but God, and out of Heaven came a message of encouragement or inspiration. Once, traveling home after a chemotherapy treatment at Mayo Clinic in Florida, I was feeling blue. God had pulled me aside to rest, and I wasn't doing any speaking engagements. I was feeling so unused. I couldn't teach my Sunday school class because my blood counts were too low, and I was confined to my house. As my husband drove our car down Interstate 95, I told God how unusable I felt. My personalized license plate is TESTIFY, and I was saying "God I don't even get to testify for you any more. I don't deserve to have TESTIFY for a license plate." Suddenly my husband said, "Look out the window!" When I did, my eyes filled with tears of joy. A man was riding beside us waving, pointing to the back of the car, and giving the thumbs up sign, saying good job! God sent a stranger on Interstate 95 to encourage me. I knew immediately this was a message straight from God, the great Encourager. Needless to say, my entire attitude changed to gratitude and joy for the awesome God we serve.

Another time God greatly encouraged me was during a speaking engagement. The air conditioner had broken, and it must have been eighty-five degrees in the church. The congregation was hot and restless. Each person was stone-faced, expressionless, and it appeared the message was not being received. As I spoke about the love of God, I prayed, "Lord, help me!" When I closed and stepped down from the pulpit, a heavenly sound filled the church. The song "Holy Spirit You Are Welcomed in This Place" burst through the sound system with such intensity that all of us in the congregation looked up expecting to see a heavenly choir. Smiles touched each face, hearts felt God's embrace, and we were all keenly aware that God had manifested His presence in a miraculous way.

Take a moment now to reflect on the times God has encouraged you. Maybe it was through a card that ministered to your heart or a bird singing sweetly in the morning hours, or maybe it was in such an obvious way that it had "from God" written all over it. Make the effort to look through your spiritual eyes to see God encouraging you, because He is.

He Is Listening

——— ❧ ———

Soon after my son went off to college, I received a distressing telephone call from him. I listened to his words and heart, and I offered words of motherly wisdom to no avail. I offered words of comfort that weren't received, and then he hung up with the attitude that I had not heard a word he said, that I didn't give him any direction or guidance. He had no more peace when he ended the call than he did before he called.

This conversation reminds me of my prayer life sometimes. I cry out to God, telling Him all that is wrong. He listens, but I don't think He has heard me. He gently guides and directs me, but I am complaining too much to hear Him. He tries to comfort me, but I refuse His peace. So when I get up from my knees I feel like my son did, but just as I heard my son's words and heart, my heavenly Daddy heard mine—even clearer. He is always listening. He is listening to our hearts even when we aren't speaking. His ear is always tuned to the cries of His children.

If you are a parent, you know that when your children are in trouble you want to rescue them immediately. But you realize some tests and trials they must work through so they can learn. The Lord wants to come to our aid immediately, but sometimes He waits in order for us to grow in faith and trust in Him. Just remember, He is listening.

One late afternoon, I was in the den on my knees before the Lord. I was crying out in a repentant prayer, asking God to take all the trash out of my life, to haul off the garbage. Then unexpectedly, my daddy walked into the kitchen and shouted, "Cindy, do you want me to haul off your trash." Wow! You can imagine how I felt, asking my heavenly Father to haul off the trash, then my earthly daddy came in and asked me that! It was an awesome moment, and I knew Daddy God was listening. Talk to Him right now. He is listening!

TRUST

Have you ever felt God was calling you to pass over to the other side? I have many times. I've felt like the disciples who Jesus told to get into the boat and go to the other side, only to get part way there and the winds of adversity begin to blow and the waves of trouble come crashing in. However, Jesus calmed the storm immediately when they called out to Him for help. He will do the same for us today. He controls the winds and storms of life. We must totally trust Him.

During one of the come-to-the-other-side experiences, the Holy Spirit gave me a poem titled "Trust."

TRUST

The bridge was swinging
Above the valley below,
With weakened ropes and
A sign that said, "Don't Go!"

To the world the bridge
Couldn't be passed,

It was too weak and the
Boards wouldn't last.

But the Master spoke, "Trust Me and
Come to the other side.
There is no other way but to trust
And abide."

Without hesitation I took the
First step,
And never looked down into
The valley's depth.

The boards cracked, some broke
As the rugged bridge swang.
But with my eyes on the Master
I lifted my voice and sang.

Immediately, I was on the other side,
Safely in my Master's arms.
Then I looked to see the way the
World said would bring me harm.

There was no swinging bridge,
No danger at all.
It was only the world's fear that
Shouted I would fall.

Then He said, "Well done, My child, with
Trust I crown your head.
You didn't listen to the world
You trusted me instead."

When we trust, we are resting upon the Savior. Look at the word †*rus*†, surrounded by the *cross* of Jesus.

Read Mark 4:35–39 and let the Lord speak, "peace, be still," to your heart and situation.

Rest and rely upon the Savior. Trust!

In a Hole

No matter the circumstances of our lives, God is always aware of where we are and what we need, even when we feel as if we have been dropped into a hole and forgotten. Read about Jeremiah's prison experience recorded in Lamentations 3:52–66.

I got to this point in June 1995. I felt so alone and helpless. I was in a state of financial destitution, and I didn't know what to do. I couldn't work due to my health, and the bills were mounting. I had prayed and prayed, but no answer came. I had applied for disability, but had not heard whether I would be approved or not. At 1:00 A.M., I was in my prayer closet praying, and this poem came to me.

In a Hole

Have you ever felt as if you have
Been dropped in a hole?
No one saw, so no one
Is told.

So, day after day, you look
For a way out.
But you see no doors or help
Just fear and doubt.

Finally, when you are tired and
You lay down to pray,
"Lord, where are you, I
Have been calling everyday?

I dug a hole and fell in,
Now I can't get out!"
Suddenly I heard a voice say,
"With faith and patience,
Not fear and doubt.

Be still and know that I
Am God, wait on me."
"Then day by day you will
Begin to see.

And you will realize I
Knew all along.
I was there with you,
You were never alone."

Exactly six hours later, at 7:00 A.M., I received a call from the disability office that my claim had been approved. I later found out the doctor had signed the paperwork just four days before. God was truly listening the entire time and was working everything out, every detail. I had hoped to get back pay from the time I applied but it wasn't approved. I had a bill of over $700 due, and a woman called me to go see her. I thought she wanted me to pray for her, but instead, she gave me a check in the exact amount of the bill due! God always provides, and you are never alone. He is there with you wherever you are. As He spoke to Jeremiah, "fear not," he is speaking to you. He is with you always regardless of how you feel! Praise the Lord!!

Jesus, My Mountain Climber

Have you ever felt so weary in your spirit and body that you didn't think you could go on? I have, and it is a terrible state to be in. Sometimes we can move to this position quickly, while other times it may be a process of days, months, or even longer. The journey appears to get harder, and the strength and courage to go forth seem to disappear.

When this happened to me, I had been in a battle for months. I knew the cancer had returned, and I was growing weaker daily, both spiritually and physically. Late one night the Holy Spirit spoke a word to me, *endurance*, then He led me through the scriptures.

These are the promises He imparted into my spirit.

Behold, we count them happy which endure. (James 5:11)

Blessed is the man that endureth temptation: for when he is tried, he shall receive the crown of life, which the Lord hath promised to them that love Him. (James 1:12)

Thou therefore endure hardness, as a good solider of Jesus Christ. (2 Tim. 2:3)

But watch thou in all things, endure afflictions. (2 Tim. 4:5)

Wherein ye greatly rejoice, though now for a season, if need be, ye are in heaviness though manifold temptations: That the trial of your faith, being much more precious than of gold that perisheth, though it be tried with fire, might be found unto praise and honor and glory at the appearing of Jesus Christ: Whom having not seen, ye love; in whom, though now ye see him not, yet believing, ye rejoice with joy unspeakable and full of glory. (1 Pet. 1:6–8)

Faith, hope, and joy began to rise up in me. The joy of the Lord instantly gave me strength to endure. I immediately went outside and stood in my yard and praised the Lord. As I looked up, only one star was shining through the clouds. I praised and praised the Lord, dancing before Him, rejoicing. Then suddenly, I noticed every star in the sky was lit up. It was the most beautiful night sky I'd ever seen. I said, "God, you turned every light on so I would know you were home!" And He spoke back to me, "I want you to shine as bright as the stars in the universe."

The Lord gave me the strength to endure hopefully, cheerfully, and to know that I wasn't on this journey alone. If He chose not to remove the mountain of suffering that lay ahead, He would take me over it. That is how I came to know Jesus as my mountain climber.

JESUS, MY MOUNTAIN CLIMBER

When I thought I had reached the limits of my endurance

Gently, Jesus whispered, *Not yet my child*,
with encouraging assurance.
Don't be frightened by the mountain
You must climb.
We will go over each rock one
Step at a time.
He fastened me securely to Him so
I wouldn't fall.
And said, *Don't listen to the world*,
focus on Me and hear My call.
As we began up the mountain, His voice
was peace and directions clear,
And I understood this mountain must be
Climbed—it wouldn't disappear.
When the winds of adversity began to
Violently blow,
He sheltered me under His wing until
He commanded them to go.
He renewed my strength with
Each step I took,
And I soon began to feel
Like the eagles look.
Soaring without effort on
The strength of the Lord.
Feeling His heartbeat in mine
And our spirits in one accord.
Thought this journey up may
Seem long, it's the sweetest
I've ever climbed.
Because, Jesus is my mountain
Climber, just one step at a time.

Whenever you feel weary, call upon your mountain climber, Jesus. He will give you the strength to endure, and together you can take one step at a time.

TO TELL HIS STORY

Thank you, Lord, for the burning
Desire that flames within my soul.
To tell the story of my Savior, the
Greatest story told.

The Son of God who came to preach,
To heal the sick and save the lost.
He knew the price He would pay for us
His life was the cost.

He bore our sins on the cross, He died
So we could live.
On that cross He suffered for us, for
The greatest gift to give.

Then God raised Him up from the dead, in
Heaven He now reigns.
The Lord of Lords, the King of Kings
The greatest story remains.

This truly is the greatest love story ever told, or ever to be told, and it needs to be shouted from the rooftops and whispered in the ears of many. Ask the Holy Spirit to guide and anoint you today to share the good news with holy boldness. Someone is dying to hear. Will you be the Lord's messenger today?

Sincere Worship—Honest, Intense Love

I t comes by way of separation from the world, isolation with God, navigation by the power of His Spirit in His Word, communication by His Spirit with Him, eradication of all that is not of Him, revelation into His truths and will, exhilaration from His presence and insight. Sincere worship.

As I was praying one day, I asked God how I could express my love for Him in prayer. First, I felt He said my love for Him had to be pure, honest, intense love. That is the beginning of sincere worship; then we separate and isolate and He navigates, communicates, eradicates, reveals, and exhilarates us by His Spirit.

Fellowship with God is vital to our existence; we cannot abide in Him without Him.

> I am the vine, ye are the branches: He that abideth in me, and I in him, the same bringeth forth much fruit: for without me you can do nothing. If a man abide not in me, he is cast forth as a branch, and is withered. (John 15:5–6)

Express your honest, intense love through sincere worship and feel exhilarated in His presence.

TEACHER'S PRAYER

Lord, give these children ears to listen
And to hear what is explained.
Give them wisdom to learn and the
Ability to retain.

Help them to be attentive and to recall
What they have been taught.
Show them an education is learning and
That grades aren't given or bought.

Help me to encourage, uplift and to
Love every single child.
Give me wisdom to know their needs
And the courage to always smile.

Give me understanding when they
Don't understand me.
And, Lord, give me Your eyes to
See what You see.
Amen.

If you are a parent, grandparent, or have ever been a student, you can understand the awesome task teachers are given and their responsibility to each child. One day when I asked the Lord how I could better pray for my children's teachers, the Holy Spirit gave me this little poem. Since then, I have given these words to many teachers who, in turn, have placed them on their desks to remind them to pray for guidance and help as they fulfill their duty of teaching.

Pray for our teachers and let them know how valuable they are, for they mold our future in the precious little ones they lead.

The Touch of the Master's Hand

The touch of the Master's hand
Is with power and grace.
The touch of the Master's hand
Sets healing into place.

The touch of the Master's hand
Is for everyone to feel.
The touch of the Master's hand
Calms the storm until it is still.

O Master, touch us with your
Hand, embrace us with your love.
Open up heaven's window and
Pour out blessings from above.

For Lord we know, nothing is greater
Than the touch of the Master's love.

Do you need the touch of the Master's hand on you today? Are you weary or sick in your body or maybe feeling a
little blue today? Or maybe you just need that added grace

today or to have your cup refilled? Whatever your need, the Master's touch will heal or still. There is no storm He cannot calm, there is no care that is too big for Him. He is able.

Right now, wherever you are, ask Him to embrace you with His love. Say: *Yes, Lord! All I need is You!*

Love Shines Through the Storm

I stand before you in the midst
Of my third battle with cancer since 1993
But, oh, how sweet and tender is the Lord
And the change He's made in me.

The first battle came in as a mild storm,
And God held me everyday.
The second storm looked like destruction,
But God taught me to walk beside Him all the way.

Each time the storm was over, I was
Stronger than before.
He gave me wings of eagles and
The strength to soar.

The storm that rages around me now
Looks like trouble on every side
But it only feels like a spring shower
With flowers blooming far and wide.

I hold to Jesus and steadfast in my
Faith I remain,
Cause He tells me He loves me and
Through that love He will sustain.

Look up and see the sunshine as the clouds
Pass far away,
And admire the beauty of the rainbow
And the promise of another day.

We all have storms in our lives—physical, emotional, spiritual, or financial. Sometimes it seems as if the storms, or tests, in life get a little more difficult each time, but the fact remains God never changes. He is the same God yesterday, today, and forever. Jesus told us that in this world we would have trouble but to be of good cheer. He overcame and we are overcomers because of the blood of the Lamb and the word of our testimony. Hold fast, fight the good fight of faith, and look for the rainbows; they are just behind the storm.

I Knew

As I prayed, I felt a hand
Resting upon my head.
I continue to pray as the
Holy Spirit so gently led.

I whispered in my prayer,
"Master is that you?"
His love flooded my soul.
It was Him, I knew.

His touch gave me peace and
Power in my prayers.
I felt my Master's hand, I
Knew He was there.

Jeremiah 33:3 says, "Call unto me, and I will answer thee, and shew thee great and mighty things, which thou knowest not." God is waiting to hear from you and to show you great and mighty things!

ANVIL

Place me on the anvil, Lord.
Mold me and make me like You.
Do what You have to Lord,
Do what You have to do.

I know it might not be pleasant,
I know there is a price to pay.
Try me, test me, make me pure,
So I can hear You say,

"Your heart is pure, Your mind is
Clean, Your soul belongs to me."
And in My Father's house you will
Reign forever—for eternity.

I prayed this prayer with fear and trembling, but I knew the only way I could be changed to be more like Jesus was to be broken. I was afraid to go to the Potter's house, but I had great assurance because I know the Potter. He carefully and lovingly holds us as He breaks and molds us. He knows the perfect temperature the fire needs to be to burn away all that is impure, and He makes us into useable vessels. Many times in our lives, we may be sent back to the Potter's house, but rest assured, we are destined to bring Him glory if we are yielding and obedient.

LET'S TALK

———— ❧ ————

Can you imagine if your child only
Came to you when he needed something?
Of course, you would listen and help, because
He pulls on your heartstrings.

But the joy, when he comes to you with
A word of love and just wants to talk.
The feeling of warmth comes rushing
In with hand-in-hand walks.

Think of our Heavenly Father and
How He must feel
When we only come to Him wanting
Something or trying to make a deal.

Isn't it time to hold His hand and
And go for a walk,
To take the time to show our love
And say, "Father, let's have a talk."

The Lord has used my children to teach me many lessons. Many times, the way they take me for granted is the same way I treat my Father. Recently, He revealed this to me when I was complaining to Him about how the children were behaving badly and being self-centered. Instantly, the Holy Spirit spoke to me, because their actions had been a reflection of mine to the Father. It was as if I were looking in a mirror; I didn't like what I saw. I had been guilty of expressing my wants and not my love. Isn't it time to take His hand and go for a walk and have a child-to-Father talk?

Going Home

God is so good not to tell us the
Trials and suffering we will endure.
Instead He builds our faith, step-
By-step He reassures.

Victory after victory we can hear
Him cheering us on!
Soon, My little child, your steps
Will lead you home.

For when you suffer for Me, your
Battles are already won.
You have a place with Me,
The Father and the Son.

Jesus said, "Let not your heart be troubled: ye believe in God, believe also in me. In my Father's house are many mansions: if it were not so, I would have told you. I go to prepare a place for you" (John 14:1–2). No matter where you are today, whether you are in the midst of battle or walking in the triumph of victory, remain steadfast knowing your steps lead home, to our eternal hope.

Empty Tomb

There is a place to go when
Everything else is closed.
We can go to the empty tomb
Where our Savior arose.

We can go to this place in our
Time of prayer.
And feel God's presence and
Power there.

He is alive—is the message we
Hear and feel so strong.
Knowing the tomb is empty and
Heaven is His home.
We rejoice with His Spirit, the
Comforter now resides.
To remind us every second
He lives, He is alive!

Every day of the year we should celebrate our risen Savior. The words *He lives! He lives!* should burst forth from our lips, from the depths of our soul, sounding as a trumpet shouting, *He lives! The tomb is empty!*

We have so much to celebrate. Tell someone today: *He lives.*

Do You Want to Lead?

So many people want to be leaders,
But do they want to serve?
Do they seek the needs of others, or
Is it the position they think they deserve?

To be a leader is to take the path
Of the needy, that is the road to follow.
To deny self and selfish wants, one
Must be willing to swallow.

Do you want to be a leader? Then
Pick up your cross and go.
Carrying the burdens of others as
God leads you to do so.

Your cross may get heavy, and when
You feel the need to rest,
You will know God's presence and the
Weight will seem less.

And at the end of the road, when
Your mission is complete,

You will hear His voice,
Well done My child, come sit at your Master's feet.

Jesus gave us a beautiful example of serving others when He washed the feet of His disciples. His life exemplifies the meaning of servitude. He led the way through service to others all the way to the cross where He laid down His life so we could live.

Jesus said, "Follow Me." He told us we must pick up our cross, and to bear the burdens of others. If you want to lead others to Christ, begin with serving others in the name of Christ.

Can you think of someone today to whom you could offer a helping hand or a kind word? Let the world see Jesus in you through what you do.

GOING THE DISTANCE

Truck drivers have a reputation
On the highways.
They are known for helping the broken
Down, during the night or day,
Whoever needs help along
Life's highway.

They are noticed by all who see them
On the road,
And people love to follow them as they
Carry someone else's load.

Every turn they take is carefully
Thought out.
Every direction they take is planned with
No room for doubt.

The force that moves them is powerful
And strong.
They always know where they are going,
And their last stop is home.

Who was just described in the message
Above?
Was it a truck driver or a Christian,
Showing God's love.

Have you ever been traveling on an interstate, following an eighteen-wheeler, then realized you were part of a convoy? If you are like me you have. There is just something about following a big truck that attracts us. There seems to be a sense of safety about them. Normally, truck drivers will stop to assist someone in need. Isn't that really the way Christians are?

I have a friend who is a truck driver, and before he came to know Christ as His Savior, the Lord gave me this poem for him. Now he is a truck-driving Christian. Praise the Lord!

We, too, have a powerful force that moves us, the power of the Holy Spirit, so let's keep on trucking until we make it home.

BEHOLD

Behold, I come quickly, I say in My Word.
Be ready and waiting, watching for Me.
Pray without ceasing, worship Me in spirit,
Do good and spread My light for all to see.

Behold, I come quickly, this I say in present
Tense, I am on My way.
Although you know I am coming you know
Not the hour or the day.

Have your lamps burning, filled with
My oil and let My light shine.
So the world will know you are My
Chosen, you are Mine.

Behold, I come quickly, My
Return is very near.
The fields of harvest are ready
Spread My truth for them to hear.

Behold, I come quickly, unannounced, I
Return like a thief in the night.
In a twinkling of My eye you will
Behold My glory in splendor and might.

I am your reward in heaven, your
Home for eternity.
Behold, I come quickly, prepare
And watch for Me.

One spring morning, as I was washing dishes and looking out of my kitchen window, a hummingbird came up to the feeder but the feeder was empty. He quickly checked for the nectar and was gone. Immediately, the Holy Spirit spoke to my heart, "Behold, I come quickly; keep your lamp burning!"

Jesus told us in the parable of the ten virgins, recorded in Matthew 25, to keep our lamps trimmed, full of oil, because we know not when the Bridegroom cometh. Stay alert and be ready!

COME HOME

I am listening, my child,
I hear your cry.
I am so close to you.
Do not pass Me by.

Come to Me, and listen to what I say.
Come as you are, and I will change your way.

I will wipe off the dirt, just as you would
wash a child of your own.
Let Me change you, accept My love
And please come home!

Our Father tells us He takes no pleasure in the death of
the wicked, but wants all to accept His Son as Lord and
live. There are so many people who still have passed Him
by, so many who have not come home. We are His children
and His desire is for none to perish.

Is there someone you know who is lost? Pray for them
to come home. Tell them about how Jesus cleansed your
sins and set you free. Hurry, before it is too late.

I Have Jesus

I may not have health, I may not have
wealth but, oh, the riches I hold.
In the hand of my Lord who gives me
Strength, provides my needs, He's the
Keeper of my soul.

He is my refuge and my fortress. On
Him, the Rock, I stand.
Though winds may blow and trouble come,
I rest securely in His hand.

Jesus is my Lord, He is my King
He is my everlasting light.
He shines through my darkest hour and
Keeps me strong in the power of His might.

Nothing in this life matters except our relationship with
the Lord. In Matthew 6:19–21, we read,

Lay not up for yourselves treasures upon the earth, where
moth and rust doth corrupt, and where thieves break

through and steal: But lay up for yourselves treasures in heaven, where neither moth nor rust doth corrupt, and where thieves do not break through nor steal: For where your treasure is, there will your heart be also.

It matters not if we are rich in wealth or blessed in health as long as Jesus is Lord of our lives, for we are truly blessed people.

What God Can Do

It's not what you can do for God
But what God can do through you.
He sees your biggest weakness as
An opportunity to work through.

He takes all your flaws and inabilities
And applies His power and grace,
To work through impossible situations
To meet Him face to face.

He equips you with His Spirit, His
Wisdom and His might,
To conquer over evil, to have
Victory in the fight.

Because greater is He who is in
You than he who is in the world.
Be that special oyster that brings
Forth precious pearls.

Do you ever think, I can't do that; I am too inadequate? Me, too, all the time, but the Holy Spirit gently reminds me that God's grace is sufficient and we can do all things through Christ Jesus who strengthens us.

If we could do what God calls us to do out of our own sufficiency, then He wouldn't call us into the work, because He wouldn't receive the glory. He works through our weakness to show forth His strength. He calls us to the impossible task where only He holds the possibility.

Look at the lives of Moses, Joseph, David, Peter, and Paul, just to name a few. It was God who accomplished the work through their lives as they yielded to Him.

Remember in all your inadequacy God is more than adequate. Yield to His will and allow Him to do the impossible. "For it is God which worketh in you both to will and to do of his good pleasure" (Phil. 2:13).

His Work Is Always Perfect

As I look above the mountain
And watch the ravens soar
The peace of God floods my soul
From heaven's opened door.

A sweet, cool breeze is blowing
And lifts my spirit high.
The presence of my Lord is here
And His angels are standing by.

Softly I heard my Master say,
Look my child at what I have done.
My work is always perfect and
In you I've just begun.

We have an awesome promise to claim for our lives in Philippians 1:6, "Being confident of this very thing, that he which hath begun a good work in you will perform it until the day of Jesus Christ." Yes! Yes! Yes! Doesn't this make you want to shout? We can be confident that God will complete the work in our lives that He began. Praise the Lord! Thank Him for that right now and have a glorious day in Christ Jesus.

Angels

White, fluffy clouds dancing by,
Painting pictures against a
Bright blue sky.

Heaven's rays beam down
From above.
Angels on missions ministering
God's love.

Look up towards heaven,
Way up high.
Was that a cloud or an angel
That just passed by?

I pray for traveling mercies every time I get in my car, and I know God's Word tells us that His angels protect us. Psalm 91:11 says, "For he shall give his angels charge over thee, to keep thee in all thy ways." I am sure you have witnessed this for yourself. Near misses, those times when you were sure a car was going to hit you. You know it was a miracle that you were spared, only seconds or inches away

from harm's way. Well, we may never know in this lifetime all the times God's angels were sent to intervene on our behalf, but we can remain forever thankful that He is indeed protecting His children.

What Do You Hear Me Say

Lord, what do you hear me say
When I lift my voice to pray?

Do you hear words of thanksgiving
And praise, or "give me, give me"
All of my days.

Lord, do I ask for what I need,
Or do you hear selfish pleas?

Lord, do you receive fellowship
And love or do I take for granted
Your power above.

Lord, help me to earnestly pray
To request my needs and thank you
For each day.

Some days I am so guilty of rushing into God's presence and telling Him all I need or think I need without praising Him first. In Psalm 95:2, we read, "Let us come before his presence with thanksgiving and make a joyful noise unto him with psalms." Psalm 100:4, says, "Enter into his gates with thanksgiving, and into his courts with praise: be thankful unto him, and bless his name."

Our praises to God usher us into His presence and He inhabits the praises of His children. Welcome the King of Glory into your heart and prayers today with praise and thanksgiving.

Cleansing Waves, Our Savior Saves

As I sit and watch the waves roll in,
I think of Jesus' blood covering all
My sin.

The beach is forever being cleansed
By the ocean waves, like our Lord
Cleansing our souls, our Savior
Saves.

The magnificent
ocean extends further
Than my eye can see, like God's
Love pouring from Him to me.

That Christ may dwell in your hearts by faith; that ye,
being rooted and grounded in love, may be able to com-
prehend, with all saints, what is the breadth, and length,
and depth, and height; and to know the love of Christ,
which passeth knowledge, that ye might be filled with
all the fullness of God. (Eph. 3:17–19)

God is love and, "God commendeth his love toward us, in that, while we were yet sinners, Christ died for us. Much more then, being now justified by his blood, we shall be saved from wrath through him" (Rom. 5:8, 9).

The ocean extends farther than our eyes can see, and God loves us more than we can grasp. As those waves roll in and cleanse the beach, Jesus' blood was shed for you and me and cleanses us from our sins. He is our righteousness.

Today, take time to meditate on God's love for you. Ask Him to reveal the length, width, depth, and height of His awesome love.

Let Jesus In

Children running and laughing
Couples hand in hand,
Do they stop to thank You
For creating this land?

Do they look at the ocean
And the wonder of it all?
Do they feel the burning
Desire to spread the gospel
Like Paul?

Or are they lost in a world
Of Satan's sin?
Lord, help them, bring
Them in!

Do you ever feel impressed to pray for people you see, people you don't know? It is exciting isn't it! One summer day, as I sat on the balcony of an ocean front hotel and watched people walking and playing on the beach, the Lord spoke to my heart that many of those souls were lost. I felt burdened to pray for everyone I saw. Some of the prayers were so detailed that I knew the Holy Spirit was interceding for a specific need in the person's life. It was an amazing experience, and before I realized it, I had spent the entire day in prayer for others. I was blessed with unspeakable joy and felt full of glory.

Today as you go out among the world, pray for salvation and blessing for God's people.

The Thirteenth Floor

Have you ever noticed in an elevator
There is no thirteenth floor.
Do you know your heart has no
Doorknob, just a door?

You can pretend there is no
Thirteenth floor,
And you can pretend God
Will force open your
Heart's door.

But until you open the door
And let Him in,
You will be like the thirteenth floor
Passed by, just feeling the wind!

For many years I was like that thirteenth floor, and I refused to open my heart to let Jesus come in. I am so thankful that God didn't give up on me. I lost sight of Him, but He never lost sight of me. He pursued me and His Holy Spirit drew me to Jesus. I am forever thankful.

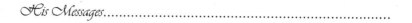

There are many people today who feel Him pass by and refuse His invitation of salvation. Let's pray for their salvation so they, too, can get on the move for Christ.

My Purpose

Lord, I know my purpose in life,
I know why I am here.
For years I questioned and wondered
But, now, the purpose is clear.

When You reached down from heaven
And saved my soul from hell,
You gave me freedom to live and
Put wind in my sails.

I live to worship You, to fellowship,
To lift my voice in praise.
To encourage others, to witness
That my Savior saves.

My life was aimless without purpose before Christ became Lord of my life. I used to often wonder what life was about and why I was a part of it, but Jesus made all the difference. He made my life have a purpose. He is the purpose. He is your purpose. He is your reason. He desires your love, your fellowship. He died for you! Yes, you! You are that important to Him. Even if you had been the only one on earth, He would have still died for you so you could live. Doesn't that give your life a purpose? He has a divine purpose for your life. "The Lord has plans to prosper you . . . plans to give you hope and a future"(Jer. 29:11). You are important and significant to His plans!

> "For I know the plans I have for you, declares the Lord, plans to prosper you and not to harm you, plans to give you hope and a future" (NIV)

HE HOLDS TOMORROW

I don't know what tomorrow holds, but
My Lord holds it in the palm of His hand.
He is already there, preparing the way,
Perfecting His plan.

Lord, make the crooked road straight,
Allow me to clearly see the way.
Help me to remain focused on You
To lean on, trust in, listen and obey.

Keep me in the center of Your will
As I seek Your face.
Help me to arrive safely in Your time
At the right place.

Thank You, Lord, for being in my
Yesterdays, today and tomorrows.
Thank You, Lord, for being tender in
My weakness and my sorrows.

In the palm of Your hand, I shall
Securely rest,
And leave all the details of my life
To You, Lord, who knows best.

Isn't it comforting to know God is the God of details. He holds all of our yesterdays, todays and tomorrows in His care. He knows where we are and how we are every second of every day. He knows us better than we know ourselves. In Jeremiah 1:5, we read, "Before I formed thee in the belly I knew thee."

Remember, He holds tomorrow, and He is taking care of every detail. After all, your name is engraved in the palm of His hand.

The Burden Rope of Tug-of-War

———— 🕊 ————

I had a vision while I was praying. I saw a woman standing with a rope in her hand. It had knots in it to represent all her burdens. Jesus held the other end of the rope. Suddenly, the woman forcefully tugged the rope. Jesus let go of His end of the rope and the woman lost her balance and fell. The rope entangled around her like chains of bondage. She looked surprised and distressed. She cried, "Lord, why won't you take these burdens from me? Why did you allow me to fall?" Jesus answered, "O My child, I only take what I have been given. I do not want what you refuse to give. I did not allow you to fall, only to fail. Each time you do, you replace in my hand another nail." As He held up His hand, she saw her name engraved in His palm. Then she heard Him say, "I paid the price on the cross; your burdens I came to bear, but only if you give them to me, not just allow me to share. Remember My child how deep my love is for you." Jesus reached down and lifted her high, and she gave Him the rope of burdens. He softly whispered, "For you I gave my life." He turned and walked away with the rope of burdens in His nail-scared hands. The tug-of-war was over, and she stood in victory, free from the burdens.

The Lord wants us to be free from the heaviness of burdens. He tells us in Psalm 55:22, "Cast thy burdens upon the Lord, and he shall sustain thee." The command in this sentence is to cast—to throw out in the direction of, like fishing; to cast a line or net. The only way the Lord can take our burdens and heaviness is if we give them to Him.

Beloved, the Lord is ready and waiting for you to release your rope of burdens. Don't get tangled and pulled down by the cares of this life; release them.

Storms and Rainbows

Some days are cloudy and full
Of gloom.
The clouds of worry weigh heavy
Full of doom.
Then the worries became reality,
Like the water in the rain,
And we wonder if we will weather
The storm again.
When it gets so bad and no sight
Of help is on the way,
Our merciful Lord sends a rainbow
To brighten the day.

Stormy days are a part of God's plan, too. The lightning deposits the needed nutrition into the soil, and the rains replenish the earth's moisture. We, too, need stormy days to strengthen us in our faith; they help us grow. The Lord controls both the winds and the rains, and He alone knows how much of both we need. You will weather the storm because Jesus is the anchor that holds.

My Heavenly Father

My eyes look up to heaven
My heart rejoices with praise!
I will sing Glory to my Father
For all of my days!
He blessed me with His Holy Spirit,
A gift only He gives.
His Spirit is alive in me,
His loving Spirit lives!
I thank Him and praise Him
I will never be the same!
I will always sing Him praises
And always acknowledge His name.

Oh that men would praise the Lord for his goodness, and
for his wonderful works to the children of men! And let
them sacrifice the sacrifices of thanksgiving, and declare
his works with rejoicing." (Ps.107:21–22)

Rejoice! We have a heavenly Father who knows everything about us, both good and bad, and He loves us anyway! Rejoice!

Why Did You Not Meet Me Today?

Have you ever given much thought to the
Time you spend in prayer?
Or do you rush to God in need when
The burden's too heavy to bear?

Do you meet Him daily with Thanksgiving
And praise in your heart?
Or do you begin your prayers with
Self right from the start?

Take time to think about what you pray
And when you meet God in prayer.
Is He calling your name because you
Forgot to meet Him there?

What would your answer be if you
Heard Him say,
"Where are you My child, why did
You not come today?"

The Lord is always waiting to hear from His children; it brings Him much delight when we fellowship with Him. One day the Holy Spirit spoke to me about the times I didn't go to my prayer closet. He revealed to me that it grieves Him deeply when we ignore His drawing and pulling us aside. I wept and repented, because I knew I had neglected the most important part of my day and the most important person in my life.

Will you meet Him today?

PRAY FIRST

How many of us decide to act
Before we pray,
To realize we need prayer to
Straighten out our way?
If we would pray to God
First for His will,
To have faith in Him, to be
Patient and still.
Decisions in life would be clear
And right.
When we stay in God's will because
His guidance is our shining light.

Wouldn't life be a lot easier if we prayed before we got ourselves in a mess instead of praying our way out of one. I've been there so many times until it is almost embarrassing. Each time it happens I think, *if I just prayed about this first, I would have done things a lot differently.* I praise the Lord for His mercy and grace to help in time of need, but let's pray first.

God's Love and Glory

Our lives are a continuous
Never-ending story.
With all pages and chapters
Full of God's love and glory.

He knew us from the beginning,
Before we were ever born.
Only He can mend the pages
Of our life that are torn.

He knows every word and all
The characters in our story.
Because He created us out of
His love for His glory.

Your life, my friend, is a love story of God's grace. Allow Him to mend all the torn pages and write "Continued in Heaven for Eternity" on the last page of your life on earth.

Until we meet again,
Cindy Beard

To order additional copies of

His Messages

please send $12.99 plus $3.95 shipping and handling to

Books, Etc.
PO Box 1406
Mukilteo, WA 98275

Or have your credit card ready and call

(800) 917-BOOK

To contact the author for speaking engagements, revivals, retreats or conferences, write:

Cindy W. Beard
His Messages Ministry
PO Box 408
Scranton, SC 29591